IKI TOTONOE

粋

IKI TOTONOE: a Japanese way of connecting with your genuine self

ISBN: 978-1-64273-315-0

Author : Saori Inagaki
Photographer : Shiori Saito (mimosa Inc.)
Designer, translatior : Mio Silvey
Translatior and editor : Scott Silvey
Printer: Toyouke Co., Ltd.
Japanese Calligrapher : Kaworu Saito

Production cooperation for the book:
Hotel - THE HARBOR TERRACE
Shrine - Morido-daimyojin
Costume - Maker's Shirt Kamakura
Others - Haruo Ohmi
- Kaori Isobedate

Photo location : Kamakura/Hayama

Printed in Japan
1 2 3 4 5 6 7 8 9 10

One Peace Books
43-32 22nd Street STE 204 Long Island City New York 11101
www.onepeacebooks.com

For a Beautiful Earth

Contents

Chapter 1
Introduction

Introduction

Japanese people have a cultural sense of beauty and values that have been built up over many years.

The Japanese often use the word ***totonoe*** (totono e) (to arrange) to describe this sense of beauty and sense of values.

I have tried to summarize the ideas we cherish based on this sense of beauty and values as habits that can be used in the modern world. And because of the chaotic world we live in these days, I hope that by incorporating Japanese spirituality into our daily lives, we can become a society in which each of us can take care of ourselves and our loved ones by preparing our minds and bodies.

I define ***totonoe*** as "connecting with yourself, right here and right now".

I believe that many people are too busy to feel the "right here and right now" in this world, often they put other people's needs before their own, and then find their hearts exhausted.

It is precisely because we live in such times that I believe it is important to consciously create moments and find items that help you to incorporate ***totonoe*** into your daily habits. It will keep your mind and body in good shape.

By taking care of yourself first, you will have more room in your heart and mind to be kind to those you love. I truly believe that if more people behave like that, the world will become a little more

totonoe

整

peaceful and kind.

Managers and leaders should especially take care of the ***totonoe***. And lead many people to happiness.

I hope you will spend more time connecting with yourself through this book. May the world be a kind and peaceful place that transcends borders.

Saori Inagaki

Chapter 2

Values we hold dear

Values we hold dear

On the soul and the body.
The most important value I hold dear is "polishing the soul and the body". I believe that the soul and the body are one, but the ways to polish the soul and the body are different.

First, let's talk about the soul.
I believe that this soul has been traveling for a long time. By having many experiences and challenges in this life, it grows and the soul is refined.

Until the moment you move on from this life, polish your soul so that it can grow to its maximum potential and feel the greatest happiness.

And this body, which you may have chosen for yourself so that your soul can grow and be the happiest it can be, is also an important vehicle for your soul.

Without this body, you would not be able to engage in the multitude of life's experiences.
Happiness, sadness, pain and joy are all important emotions that we can feel because of this body.

Hugging your loved ones is also possible because of this body.

It is the vehicle of the soul, and It can also be called a borrowed body, since everyone must return it when they move on from this life.

If it is something we have borrowed, we should use it as carefully and conscientiously as possible and return it at the end.

As if it is a book, or an object that we have borrowed from someone, we want to handle it as carefully as possible. We must also return it as cleanly as possible so that it is in the same condition it was when we borrowed it.

If this body is also something borrowed, we should treat it with as much care and reverence as possible. For this reason, we take care of our bodies inside and out. This may include things like going to doctors, dentists, beauty salons and home skin care regiments.

And since our bodies are made from the food we eat, we should also be conscious of what we eat and keep ourselves healthy until we finally give it back.

Before going to bed or taking a bath, we should express our gratitude to our body by touching it from head to toe, saying "Thank you for letting me use this body today”.

If you do this consistently for a while, your body will respond positively. Many people have experienced their skin becoming more beautiful and their body becoming less tired.

I have often experienced that when I am not feeling well if I put my hands on that part of my body and say "thank you" a lot, in no time at all, I feel healed.

In Japan, there has long been a concept of ***Teate*** (te ate). When you have a stomachache, you naturally put your hand on your stomach, and when you have a headache, you naturally put your hand on the part that hurts.

When a child has a stomachache, the mother puts her hand on the child's stomach to relieve the pain.

Touch your body every day.
Tell it thank you.

Many people hurt themselves when they think that this body belongs only to them, but after thinking that this body is something borrowed, many people have come to think that they should use it with care and respect.

Ever since I can remember, I have believed that the soul and the body are separate. That the soul has chosen this body so that it can grow the most in this life. (Whether I like this body (vehicle) or not.)

So when I saw someone else, I looked at that person with a sense of "Oh, you have chosen this body this time!" I had the feeling since I was a child that I was having a conversation with the soul within that person.

That because it is this body, this soul can grow the most and be the happiest.

If that is so, then I realize that, looking at other people and thinking, "That person is beautiful and I envy her," or "I wish I had been born with looks like that person," is not very meaningful.

Your soul will not be the most shiny and polished if it enters someone else's body. It is this body that you have chosen for that soul of yours to be the most polished.

Instead of comparing yourself to someone else, one must focus on how to polish this soul and body to its brightest shine before you pass from this life. If not, life will pass by in a flash while you are comparing yourself to others.

Life goes by surprisingly quickly.

When you graduate from this life, you will have the shiniest soul possible and you will give your body back to the universe in the best condition possible.

Thinking in this way, and focusing on improving our soul and body is an important way of thinking that can make our days happy and fulfilling.

The first step is to take care of our own self-confidence.

Chapter 3

Why do people get bewildered and frustrated?

Why do people get bewildered and frustrated?

Before we can polish our soul and body, we need to ***totonoe*** which means to get in shape (prepare or tone the mind and body).

Essentially, everyone's soul is shiny and bright when they are born. When you see that innocent and clean energy of a baby, you will feel the shiny soul.

As we grow out of that state, enter society, and become adults, we encounter a variety of emotions. It is very good that you are human and have emotions.

However, as we grow older, we may get hurt by the rules of society or by someone's unkind words. We cannot express our feelings freely, so they start to accumulate.

These accumulated feelings become litter in our minds and continue to grow.

To put it in an easy-to-understand image, the dust and dirt of emotions gradually accumulate like grime around the original, sparkling, diamond-like soul.

The light of a shining soul becomes dimmed by a veil of darkness.

When this happens, it becomes difficult to recognize your true self, what you value, and what your heart is telling you.

I exist.
What do I really want to do?
What is it that I really love?

It is difficult to notice your own negative mood, so you find yourself doing things you don't want to do, or wondering why things are not going well for you. You may blame yourself for being upset and frustrated.

If this sounds like you, don't worry.
The reason for your frustration is not your fault.

It is caused by the dust and dirt of emotions that have accumulated on their own.

If you feel like you have accumulated negativity around your true self, it may be proof that you have been doing your best to keep so many emotions locked up inside of you.

Just as we clean our rooms every day, we need to first wipe away the dust and dirt of the mind that builds up inside us. Polishing, however, is more than that. The first step is to clean up the mind.

That is what I would like to talk about next, preparing items and actions that you can incorporate into your daily life to ***totonoe*** your mind and body. All of them can be done immediately.

One of them is to take a morning walk and feel the beauty of nature. Look at the mountains, the ocean, the river, the sky, take a deep breath of good air, and appreciate the sun.

Be aware of the time you have to connect with your center, your heart.

Make time to feel "here and now, myself," even if it is just for a few moments.

Try to incorporate a few items and actions into your daily life that make you feel good, happy, and content.

By consciously taking a little time to connect with your center, you will become more aware of your heart's voice.

Emotional dust accumulates every day.
By making time to adjust each day, you can keep your soul and body shiny and clean so that they don't become increasingly more soiled.

Also, tears can wash away the built-up emotional dirt all at once. So, cry when you are sad. Cry when you are frustrated. Tears of joy are also good. Please do not hold back when you want to cry, but let your tears flow. By doing so, your soul will be cleaned and polished again.

If you can make time to adjust every day in this way, the emotional refuse will disappear more and more. You can return to the original diamond-like brightness of your soul. It will be easier to recognize what you want to do, what you like, or what you don't like, what your heart says.

Once you get to that point, you will be able to find many of your strengths and challenge yourself to do more and more of the things you like. Your soul will respond by becoming more polished and thus moving more joyfully through the world.

Let's start by getting in shape.
Let's start from the place where you are ready.

Chapter 4

Time-Specific Objectives to "*Totonoe* Everyday"

Time-Specific Objectives to "*Totonoe* Everyday"

In Japan, there are many events and objects that have long been used to prepare the mind. By continuing to do so, Japanese people have been able to adjust our minds and strengthen our spirits.

In Japan, there exists a thing called *Do* (do u) which means the way, the path, method, discipline.
For example, calligraphy, flower arrangement, and Judo cannot be mastered unless one is able to keep oneself in order, or follow the *Do*.

I will show you how to ***totonoe*** (manifest order in your daily life), so please just start with what feels comfortable to you. And most importantly, enjoy yourself.

Totonoe is to experience yourself in the present moment. To feel here and now, myself.

Some ways you may experience this could be to wake up 30 minutes or an hour earlier than usual, take a morning walk, make a cup of green tea for yourself, take a long bath while your children are sleeping, and so on. Take in the items and actions that fit your individual life and make time to feel "here and now, myself".

By making this little time, you will see a great change and much more joy in your future.

Let's consider the right items and actions for you in the morning time, afternoon time, and evening time.

First, let me explain the purpose.

***Totonoe* in the morning time.**

The purpose of morning time is "to be thankful".
When you wake up, start with gratitude for waking up today.
That your heart is beating.
That you can breathe.
Your blood is flowing.
None of these things you can control. Also, in this moment we can feel that we are being KEPT alive rather than simply being alive.

In addition, when you thank yourself for waking up today.
If your loved ones and family are also awake, be even more thankful.
Everything in our day-to-day should not be taken for granted. It is a miracle that you and your loved ones wake up every day.

We live in a series of miracles every day.

The morning time is "to be thankful".
Start the day with gratitude.

Totonoe during the daytime.

The purpose of daytime is "to grow our souls".

During the daytime, you can work, do housework, interact with people in your personal life, cook, do laundry, and complete tough tasks at work. Because of this body, you can take on these challenges, feel a variety of emotions, and your soul can grow again.

These challenges exist because they are there for you.

All of your roles and work will refine your soul, so keep challenging yourself.

The goal of the daytime is to "grow your soul".

Totonoe at night.

The purpose of night time *totonoe* is to say "Thank you".
This is the time to say "thank you" to your body for its hard work throughout the day.
For example, while massaging your body in the bath or before bed, touch it with your hands from head to toe and tell it thank you for letting you use it today.
It is because of this body (vehicle) that we can have many experiences. Give many thanks to this body, which is also the vehicle of our soul.
With those words, it will do its best again tomorrow.

The purpose of the night time is "to say thank you".

How many times have you said thank you to yourself today?

Now let me introduce you to some items and actions that will help you get ready for the next step.

Chapter 5

Let's start *totonoe* today

1. Start the day with "Thank God/ the universe/ or whatever you believe for the miracle of waking up"

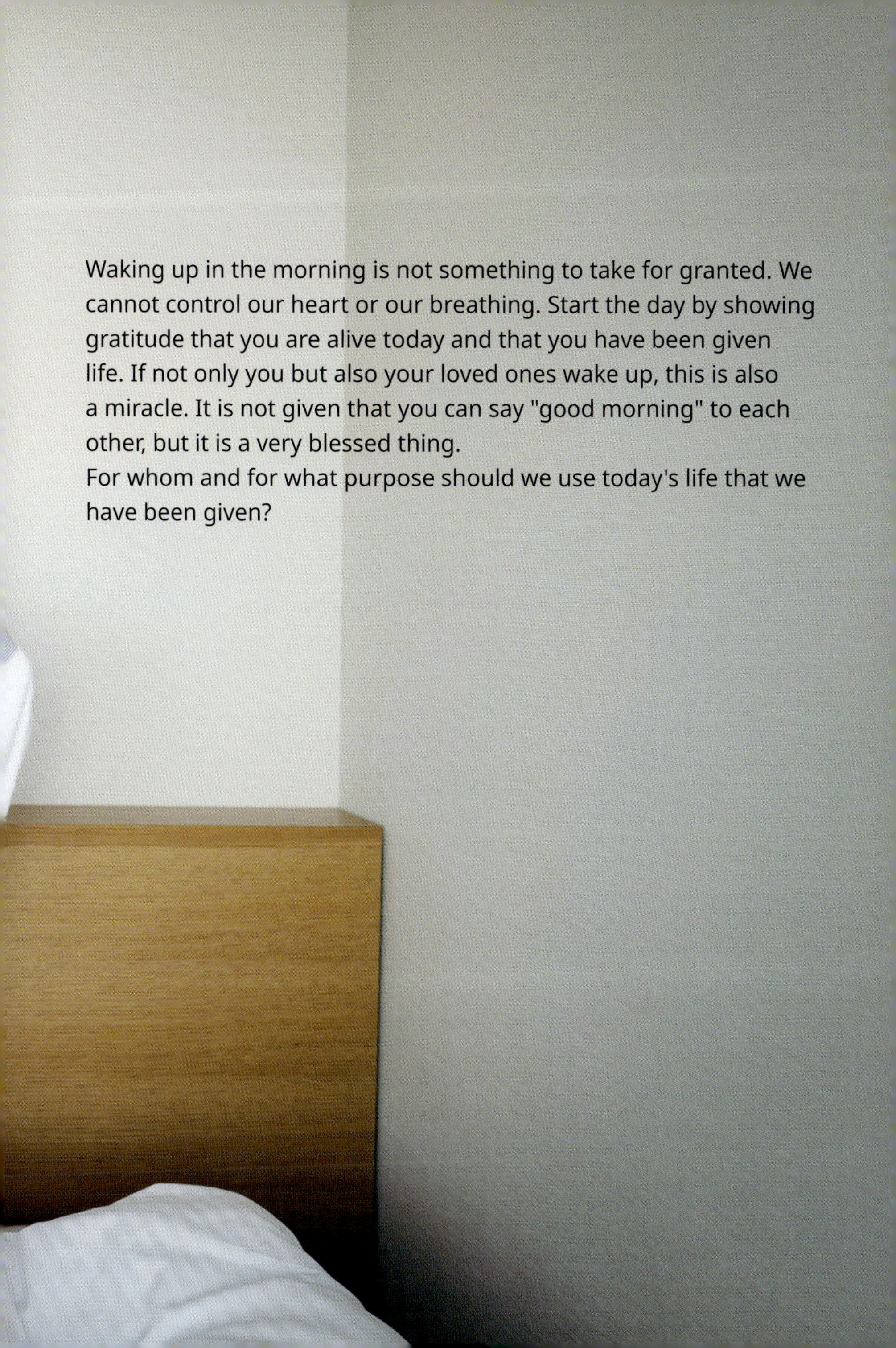

Waking up in the morning is not something to take for granted. We cannot control our heart or our breathing. Start the day by showing gratitude that you are alive today and that you have been given life. If not only you but also your loved ones wake up, this is also a miracle. It is not given that you can say "good morning" to each other, but it is a very blessed thing.

For whom and for what purpose should we use today's life that we have been given?

2. When you wake up, open the curtains and enjoy the morning sun

When you wake up, adjust your bed, open the curtains, and take in the morning sun. Getting the morning sun as soon as you wake up helps to balance your mind with the secretion of serotonin. Morning sun exposure and mental balance are connected.

Since morning sun exposure resets the body clock for the day, it also facilitates the secretion of melatonin at night, which helps you get a good night's sleep.

Don't forget to be grateful to the sun as well.

3. Take a deep breath and imaging the day

Meditate and take a slow, deep breath.
This is a time for imagining how you will treat your mind and body for the day, and what and for whom you will use the life you have received. It is an important time to adjust your actions and mindset for the day.

4. Activate your cells with your own words

In the morning, when you get ready and look in the mirror, say to yourself, "Okay! Let's have fun today!" Say the words aloud that will cheer up your heart.

Your words are heard best by you, with your ears. What words do you always say to them? Let's cherish and respect the power of words, the "spirit of speech". Using positive words to speak to yourself will raise your positivity overall.

5. Put your hands together to give thanks

Give thanks to the universe. Start the day with a sense that we are not living by ourselves, but that we are being kept alive.
Let us give thanks for the protection we have received today.
In Japan, since ancient times, people have cherished the custom of expressing their gratitude to the unseen, invisible and higher beings by placing their hands together at shrines, temples, Kami-dana (Shinto altars), and Butsudan (a Buddhist altars).
The truly important things are the ones that are invisible to the eye.

6. Clean

Cleaning also helps to improve your mind.
Especially, the entrance to a building or space is the pathway of ch'i (vital or "animating" energy).
If the entrance is full of things or is dirty, it is believed that dirty ch'i will enter the room through the dirty place. Always clean the entranceway of your home to let good ch’i into the house.

7. Make *Matcha*
(a traditional Japanese powdered green tea)

Get up a little earlier than usual and spend 10 minutes carefully making a cup of tea for yourself.

In Japan, the tea ceremony was originally a hobby enjoyed by samurai warriors. They who valued it as a time to unify their spirit and face themselves, as well as a time to calm their minds and relax.

Matcha tea contains a variety of ingredients such as dietary fiber, various vitamins and minerals, polyphenols, and caffeine. All of these properties make it the perfect drink to elevate your body and spirit.

Cherish the quiet time to prepare your mind and body, the beginning of your day. Just by making this small amount of time, you will feel more ***totonoe*** every day and will change the way you live from then on.

8. Take a morning walk

Take a 15-30 minute walk within an hour of waking up. While taking a walk or exercise, the morning sun will further activate the secretion of serotonin. This is a recommended action to regulate the mind and body.

Be grateful for a body that can take a morning walk and for the beauty of nature.

Be a person who can feel a lot of happiness every day.

9. Purify your surroundings with salt

In Japan, it has long been said that salt purifies the defiled and invites good luck.
Salt is considered precious and sacred. Placing salt on a Shinto altar or heaping salt in a house or store can bring good ch'i into the home or other area. It is also used to ward off bad luck and negativity.

Since heaping salt absorbs negativity, it should be changed at least twice a month. In Japan, the first day of the month and the 15th day of the month are the days to replace old salt. The 1st being the beginning of the month and the 15th being the fullness of the moon, which is believed to be the day when we can easily connect with the gods according to Shintoism.

By adopting this custom, we can also give thanks to the place that we offen take for granted.

10. Prepare yourself while saying thank you to your body

Preparing yourself, such as putting on makeup or brushing your teeth, is a way of paying respect to your body. Get ready while saying thank you. When you are taking care of your skin, touch your skin while saying, "Thank you for everything". You will begin to notice how hard you are always working. When you look in the mirror, humbly compliment yourself a lot for your nice features.

Choose an outfit that excites you and put yourself in a good mood for the day by asking your heart what you want to wear today.

11. Eat for the mind and body

Your mind and body are made of what you eat.
What do you want to eat today? Ask yourself and choose what pleases your mind and body.
How many more meals will you have in your life? Time = life = finite.
In the time you have left, cherish the time you spend eating. Also choose who you will spend that precious time with.

Make mealtime a happy time that pleases your mind and body.

12. Rice and *Soba*

Rice and ***Soba*** (buckwheat noodles) have long been cherished by the Japanese people.

Rice

Rice has been eaten by the Japanese people since ancient times. Rice has been considered very important and sacred to the Japanese since the formation of the culture.

The sun, moon, sea, mountains, wind, rain, animals, plants, and so on are all gods in nature, as we say in Japan. Since rice cultivation is susceptible to the influence of nature, people consider it sacred, believing that the gods' power makes rice cultivation possible.

That little piece of rice contains a perfect balance of carbohydrates, protein, vitamins, minerals, fiber, and other nutrients.

In Japan, there are many festivals and events throughout the year. Many of them are rituals to pray for a bountiful rice harvest and to express gratitude for the blessings of rice.

Soba

Soba is a traditional Japanese food that has been loved since the ***Edo*** period. During the ***Edo*** period (1603 - 1867), the restaurant industry flourished as many men migrated to ***Edo*** alone. It is said that the noodle-like buckwheat noodles that are cut into thin strips and eaten today were born in the early Edo period.

The three major fast foods that were popular in that *Edo* period were soba, tempura, and sushi.
Among these, soba was extremely popular because it was cheap and quick.
Soba is rich in vitamin B1 and dietary fiber and low in calories, making it a good choice for beauty and health.

In Japan, people also end the year by eating "New Year's Eve *soba*" on New Year's Eve.

It is a wish for longevity, to live as long as the length as the *soba* noodles.

13. Eat seasonal foods

Each season provides nourishment specific to that time of year. Nourish your mind and body with seasonal foods.

Spring

Japanese people eat bamboo shoots and butterbur sprouts (young flower buds of a native, leafy perennial) in the spring. It is a joyful way to feel the arrival of spring in your mind and on your tongue.

Summer

Summer vegetables are full of nutrients from the abundant sunlight. Eating cucumbers, tomatoes, and watermelons will help you to experience a deeper sense of the season.

Autumn

You will know it's the autumn season when you eat root vegetables. Mushrooms, and chestnuts that have absorbed the nutrients of the soil and are finally nearing the end of another year.

Winter

Radishes, carrots, lotus roots, and other vegetables that survive the cold and harsh winter months and store a lot of sweetness. Make winter a warm season with ingredients that go well with hot pot dishes, soups, and stews.

Seasonal ingredients allow the body to feel the blessings of nature.

Nourish your mind and body with the seasons.

14. Greetings at meals and chopsticks

When we eat a meal, we say *Itadakimasu*.
It is a word of gratitude for receiving the lives of other animals and plants to nourish our lives.

When we finish eating, we say *Gochiso sama desu*.
It is a phrase of gratitude and respect to the person who prepared the meal, as well as, the people who cultivated and harvested the food.

The Land of Chopsticks

In Japan, we eat with chopsticks.
After birth, people use chopsticks at the **weaning ceremony**, and in everyday life, people have their own set of chopsticks and use them, for many purposes.

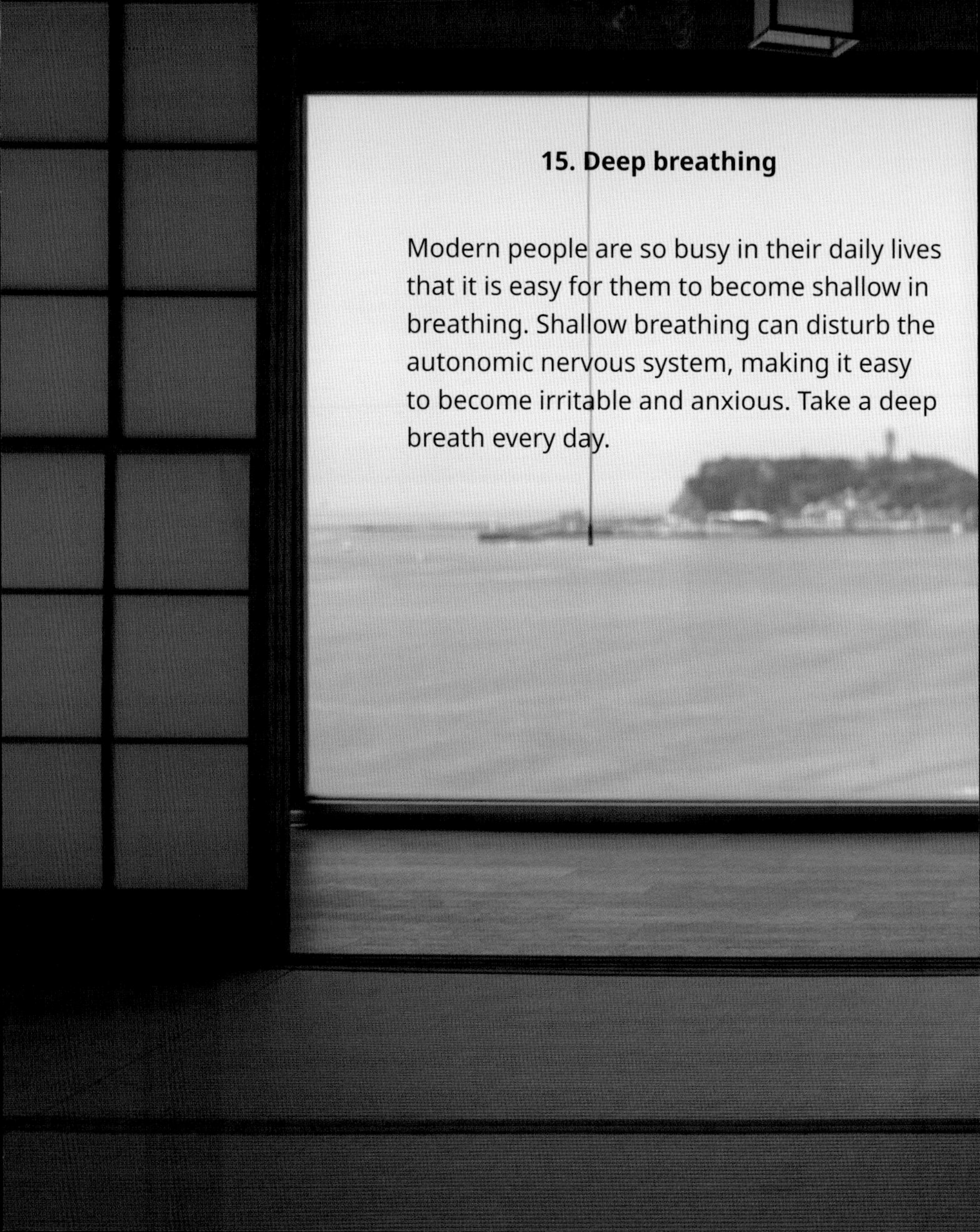

15. Deep breathing

Modern people are so busy in their daily lives that it is easy for them to become shallow in breathing. Shallow breathing can disturb the autonomic nervous system, making it easy to become irritable and anxious. Take a deep breath every day.

Make time to meditate and take deep breaths as soon as you wake up in the morning, during your lunch break, and for two minutes before going to bed at night.

Deep breathing is an important time to connect with yourself.

16. Smile

A smile has the power to energize your mind. "You don't smile because you are happy; happiness comes to you because you smile". Just as seeing a smiling person makes you feel at peace, smiling also has the effect of putting people at ease.

When you look in the mirror, smile while imagining yourself feeling happy.

Smiling makes you and your loved ones happy.

17. The Law of the *Tarai* (Tub)

A tarai is a circular container used for washing one's face and clothes. If you fill the tarai with water and push the water from your side to the opposite side, the water will return to your side from both sides of the circular container.

Conversely,
If you pull water toward you, the water will escape from the left and right sides of the circular container.

This is the same as,
If you offer good things and good words from yourself, good things and good words will come back to you in a roundabout way.

If you do something bad or offer bad words, they will also come back to you.

This is a metaphor for the fact that if you take more from others than you give, wanting more and getting more for yourself, you will move away from them.

What you do, good or bad, will come back to you.
If you want others to be kind to you, offer kindness from yourself.

Say thank you at home and at work.
Say thank you for all of the good things that are in your life.

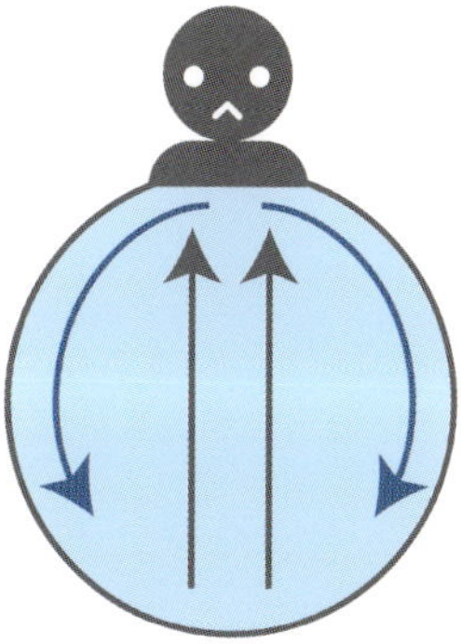

When you pull the water toward yourself, the water moves outward and away from you.

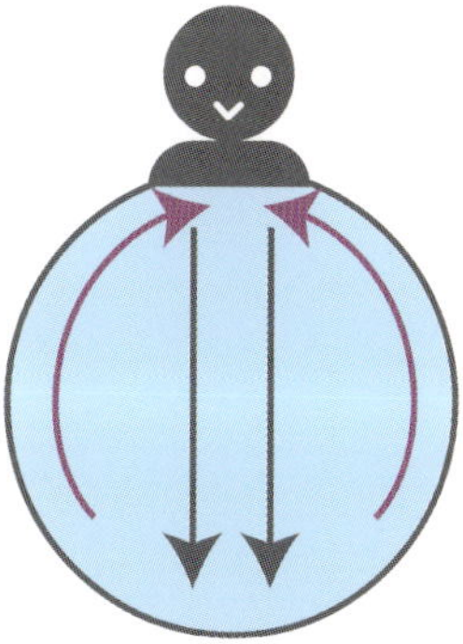

When you gently push the water away from you, the water flows back to you.

18. Pray at shrines and temples

Since ancient times, people in Japan have cherished the custom of putting their hands together to pray at shrines, temples, Kamidana (Shinto altar), and Butsudan (Buddhist altar) to express their gratitude to the unseen, higher beings. This can also be done at other sacred places or even alone in nature. What is truly important is invisible to the eye.

19. Make time to be in nature

Look at the sky every day.
Feel the beauty of nature.
No two days are the same.
Kneel down and touch the soil.
Listen to the wind in the trees and smell the scent of flowers around you.
Make time to experience nature and the beauty of the earth around you.

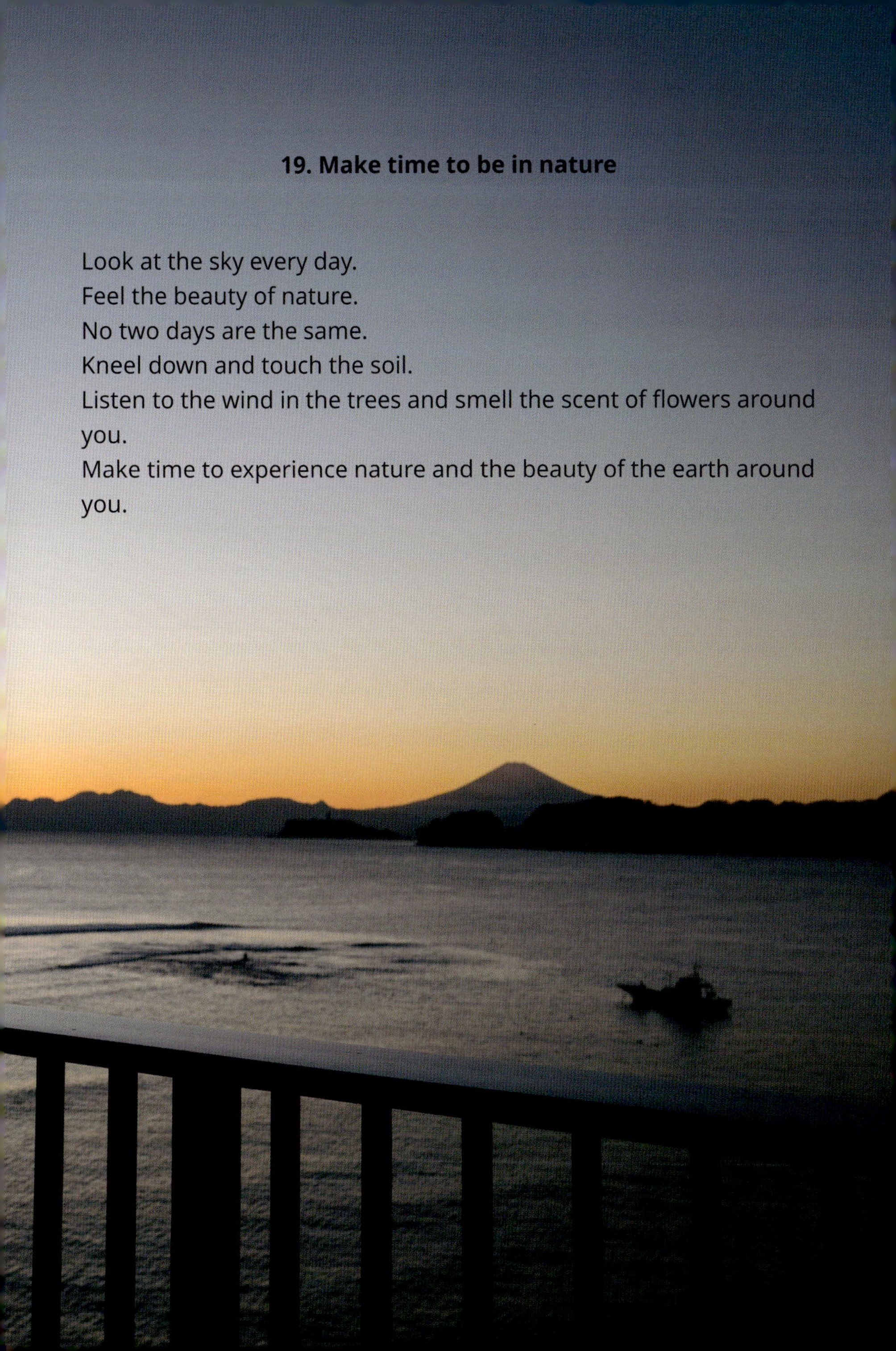

20. Cultivate your mind

Make time to experience art and culture.

In Japan, watching *Kabuki*, a traditional Japanese dramatic art form, is an opportunity to experience the beauty of the play, dance, music, and history. Going to plays, movies, poetry readings and other cultual events helps us to grow and expand our knowledge.

Visiting gardens is also stimulating.
Karesansui (dry landscape) is a style of Japanese gardens in which stones and sand are arranged without water to represent the water flow of a river through the mountains. It evokes a sense of *Wabi-*

Sabi (imperfect beauty) and *iki*, which is the unique aesthetic sense of the Japanese people. Any style of garden though is a place to find unexpected wonder and refreshment.

Looking at art and reading books, visiting museums and other cultual institutions also nourishes the mind.
Make time to unify your spirit and mind by looking more deeply at art. Beyond that, try not only look at the art but take a moment to consider the thoughts it arises in you and what "meaning" might be within the work.

21. Listen to music that makes your heart happy

When you are feeling down, happy, or lonely, use the power of music to heal your heart. Make a list of music that makes your heart happy. Music will surely cheer you up.

22. Handle Tools with Care

In Japan, people have long believed that tools have a soul of their own. Craftsmen say that if they do not handle their tools with care, they cannot do good work. The mind that appreciates and cherishes tools creates delicate and beautiful work. This thoughtfulness will be conveyed to others through your treatment of tools.

23. Bath time

Japan has a custom and culture of bathing. The presence of hot springs and abundant water are geographical reasons for this custom.

Bathing is not only a way to keep the body clean, but also way to relax both mentally and physically.

When bathing at home, make time to adjust your thoughts and mind while perhaps burning your favorite candles.

24. Say thank you to your body

Before going to bed, touch your body via massage and say thank you to your body for letting you use it today. Then, tell your body, "See you tomorrow". Your body will get better and work hard for you again. Don't forget to thank your body every day for always working hard for you, no matter what time of day it is.

25. Focus on bedding

The quality of your sleep has a lot to do with the quality of your life. Choose bedding such as pajamas, bedspreads, sheets, and pillows made of materials that feel good against your skin. Even if others say it feels good, it is important that you feel that way. Trust your own skin sensation of what "feels good" to you.

26. Gratitude before going to bed

Before you go to bed give thanks for the day.
Be thankful that you made it through the day safely, and that your loved ones made it through the day safely. Be aware that none of this is a given. In Japan, we have a saying, "Okage sama (Thanks to shadow)." It is a time to be thankful for the existence that has been supporting us in the shadows, and that we have been able to spend this day safely thanks to them.

27. Write down three things you are thankful for

Before you go to bed, think of three good things or things you are thankful for in your day and write them down in a notebook. No matter how bad your day was, there will always be something good and something to be thankful for. Even if you are having a bad day, at least before you go to bed, try to focus on what you were thankful for during the day. What were you thankful for: that you woke up, that you could breathe, that your loved ones were doing well?

Gratitude will gently cleanse your mind and increase your sense of well-being each day.

28. Incorporate your favorite things into your life

Incorporate many of your favorite things into your daily life.

For example.
One of my "likes" that I use every day is a product called "Charcoal Beauty".
It is made from burned and thinned wood from mountain maintenance into charcoal so that it is not wasted. Then I mix the charcoal powder with water and drink it as charcoal water.

This is a product that is kind to both the environment and our bodies.
By purchasing a product that cleanses our bodies and also contributes to the environment, we are making the world a better place.

Buying is a way to support a cause. What are your reasons for making purchases?

If you choose products that you use daily based on the values you hold dear, your heart will be filled with satisfaction.
Make every day full of what you love.

29. Japanese seasonal events and culture

Japan has four distinct seasons, and there are many events that allow you to experience the seasons.

Spring events

In spring, when cherry blossoms bloom Japanese people enjoy *Ohanami* (viewing cherry blossoms). They spend time with family and friends, eating bento lunches and drinking sake to celebrate the spring season while admiring the cherry blossoms. This time is a favorite of many Japanese people.

Summer events

Summer is a lively season with fun at the beaches, summer fireworks and festivals held all over the country.
Then there is ***Obon***, a custom that has been handed down in Japan since ancient times. ***Obon*** is a time to commune with and be thankful to our ancestors. It is because of our ancestors that we are here today. During this time, I think about living each day carefully and cherishing it fully.

Autumn events

In autumn in Japan, there are many festivals to celebrate the rice harvest and the harvest of fruits and vegetables.

One example is
Otsukimi (moon viewing). It also means "harvest moon".
While viewing the full moon, people pray and celebrate the harvest and fruitfulness of rice and vegetables.

The *Niinamesai*, a traditional event to thank the gods for a bountiful harvest, is also very important, at this time. Many Japanese believe this is the most beautiful time of year.

Winter events

Many events are held to look back on the year, to give thanks, and to bring the year to a close. The harvest of the year is over, and preparations for the next year's harvest begin.

You can experience Japanese culture through seasonal events and festivals.

30. Incense

Incense is another item that has been around since ancient times in Japan.
It is used not only to relax by enjoying the fragrance, but also to cleanse the space.

Choose incense of natural origin, and while ventilating the room, use your favorite fragrance to set the place and your mind at ease.

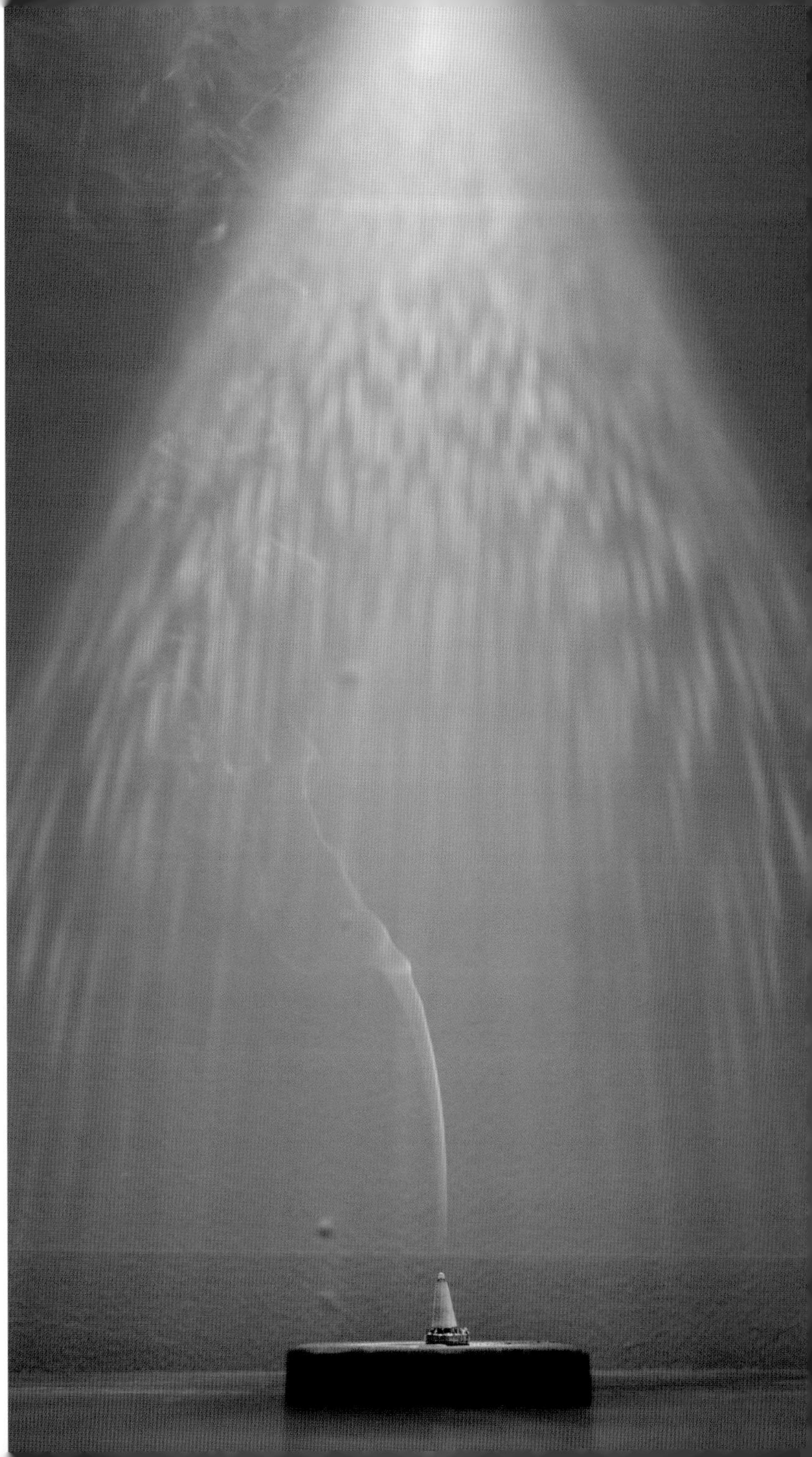

31. *Kashiwade* (clapping hands)

When people go to shrines, they clap their hands in prayer.
We also clap when we give blessings or cheer.

At shrines, it is said that clapping is used to signal to the gods that you have come to pay your respects.

It is also believed that the sound of clapping vibrates in the air and purifies the atmosphere of the place.

When you want to clear the atmosphere of a room or a place, you can do so with Kashiwa clapping hands.

32. Letters

In this digital age, handwritten letters are a welcome sight. A letter written with time and care conveys to the recipient the thoughtfulness and care that went into it. Writing a letter itself shows respect and appreciation for the recipient. Let your heart be conveyed through your letters.

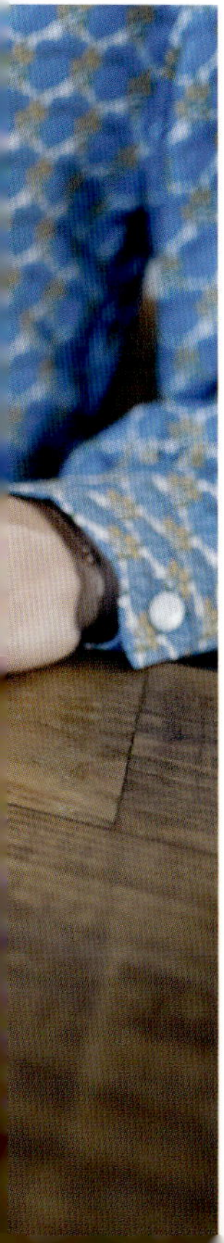

33. Decorate with flowers

Decorating with flowers is a way to take care of yourself. By decorating with flowers, you can make the space you are in more comfortable. By placing yourself in a beautiful environment, you will feel calm and relaxed. By always being aware of nature's bounty, you will be able to experience its beauty and fragrance. Most importantly, your mind will become more attuned to it.

34. Drink Hot water in the morning

In the morning, warm up your body with a cup of hot water to gently wake you up. Say "thank you" to hot water, which is good for digestion, absorption, and hydration. Start your day off on the right foot by drinking hot water for your mind and body.

THE HARBOR TERRACE

35. Incorporate symmetry

Symmetry is the quality of being made of exact or similar parts facing each other or around a central line. In nature, it is found in many living things and objects. Shapes with symmetry are stable and easy to maintain a center of gravity and balance.
It can also have aesthetic value and is widely seen in art and design.

Align your place and thinking with the laws of nature and its aesthetic value.

36. While I have this body, use words of love.

Thank you.
I'm sorry.
I love you.

These are all words of love I want to use.

Repeat these words to yourself on a daily basis.

While I still have this body.
I'll pass on lots of love.

Thank you.

感謝

Chapter 6

What you will encounter when you get in shape

What you will encounter when you get in shape

Please try to incorporate your favorite items and actions into your daily life little by little. Your mind and body will rejoice and you will feel the happiness you desire. As the number of good feelings increases, irritability and fuzziness will decrease, and you will have more room in your heart and mind.

This "space" is important.

When you have more space, you begin to notice greater beauty and appreciate things right in front of you which you did not notice before.

You see a flower blooming on the path you pass by every day and you feel happy to see how beautiful it is. But all along the way, you realize that the flower had been blooming there for many years and you had never noticed before.

When some people are frustrated, they nag at their children or hurl harsh words at their partner. As their mind becomes more organized and it has more space, they realize that it is no big deal and that the fact that they are doing well every day is a blessing. They will even start to feel gratitude.

In Japan, there are many traditions that appreciate beauty in "blank spaces".

For example, calligraphy also values the space around the

characters.
Calligraphy is said to be the art of "blank spaces".

The tea ceremony also has a lot of awareness of space.

iki

Whether it is the margins found in literature such as ***Haiku***, or the undisturbed areas found in the gardens of temples and shrines. We can feel the imagination and beauty that comes from "cutting away the superfluous".

What we can encounter because we have created a blank space in our minds by preparing ourselves is the appreciation and beauty that is already there, right in front of us.

Chapter 7
Aiming to be a person of *iki*

Aiming to be a person of *iki*

As the character *iki* means "stylish." I believe that I can become a real *iki* person at the age of 90.
Until then, I will experience various things in my life, and even if my way of life is not cool, or I am a bad person, or I am what is called a wild person, I will realize it and refine my way of life day by day to become a person with a cool way of life.
As you repeat this process of refining your way of life, when you reach the age of 90, you will become a *iki* person with a cool and beautiful way of life.

The guiding phrase is "***iki or boorish***."

The Chinese character for *iki* is composed of the numbers 9 and 10.

It is not about comparison, it is not about profit and loss, it is not about righteousness.
The guiding phrase for choosing how to live and how to be based on ***beauty*** is "*iki* or boorish".

Are the words we use *iki* or boorish?
Are my actions *iki* or boorish?
It is an important question to ask yourself.

Chapter 8

The aesthetic sense of *iki*

The aesthetic sense of *iki*

When I consider the times I feel *iki*, it is often in the realization that both I and others exist! When you think about the times you feel that sense of *iki*, it will be in the presence of other people .

When you act and speak with the other person in mind, the *caring* for the other person may be when the sense of beauty called *iki* is born.

For example, there is this story.

There was a narrow bridge over a large river. When a person was about to cross the bridge, he saw a person walking from the other side. He did not go to the bridge, but waited for the person coming from the other side, looking at the river below, to let that person cross first. He did not want the person crossing to feel that he had gone to the trouble of waiting for them to cross. He acted in such a way that the person crossing would not be bothered, as if to say, "I came here to look at this river".

Perhaps this is one *iki* way to act.

There is another famous story.

When the queen entertained a guest of honor from a certain country at a dinner party. Someone unfamiliar with Western manners drank water from the finger bowl for washing his fingers. At that time, the queen did not reprimand him, but acted as if nothing had happened by drinking water from the finger bowl herself in the same manner. It was to avoid embarrassing her guests.
It was not to pretend to be right, but to lean in.

However, I am not sure if that is really the right answer, or if she really should have taught the proper manner to the person for his/her cultual knowledge. Perhaps the answer is that there are as many answers as there are people.

I think that the way to cultivate one's sense of beauty is to live one's life by making choices while asking oneself what is the meaning of beauty, consideration and community toward others. By asking ourselves whether what we have just done was *iki* or boorish, we can realize a *iki* way of life.

Chapter 9
Finally

Finally

What we adults need to do now is
to get ourselves in order, ***totonoe***.
Take care of your own mind and be able to take care of the people we love.

If we can expand this circle,
the happiness of each and every one of us will increase.

Everyday,
what we see, what we feel, what we choose.

The choices we make create our hearts and minds.
And you will live the reality of your choices.

The answers are all within us.
To become aware of that answer.
To be in alignment and to connect with yourself.

The criteria for making a choice is
The aesthetic sense of *iki*.

I have written this book with the hope that by making choices based on the aesthetic sense within us, we can realize a society that is easy to live in, a beautiful world, and a beautiful planet for the next generation.

To you who have encountered this book
With love, gratitude and prayers.

Iki to the world!

Chapter 10

Special Thanks

Special Thanks

Takumi Kawahara
Shiori Saito
Mayumi Sada
Yuta Setoguchi

Ai Nakane
Hideki Fujinaka

Ayako Takano

Hiroshi Yamaguchi

iki-na-joshido

Mizuno Kobayashi

Rikako Matsushita

Yoshifumi Suzuki

ABC International Preschool
Ayaka Fujisawa
Azusa Yoshikawa
Emiko Terai
Hachidai Okamoto
Hideyuki Kondo
Hiroko Takahashi
Hiroko Uto
Hiromi Katsumoto
Isao Inagaki
Junko Mitarai
Kana Sugamoto
Kaori Isobedate
Kaori Ohashi
Kaworu Saito
Keiko Mizuno
Le champ des vertus Paris
Lily&Gold,Inc.
Maki Honda
Maki Kuraoka
Maki Takayama
Mari Meguro
Minoru Ogawa
Mitsu Inagaki
Miyuki Morita
Nobuko Okumura

nonno
Noriko Murata
Noriko Sugawara
Poupelle Bus in Itako
Rie Kubota
Satomi Ozawa
Shoko Ueda
Shunji Sugawara
Silk Grace Co., Ltd.
Sumie Mizumoto
Takayuki Sugawara
Tamami Curtis
Tetsuo Yamazaki
Toshio Sugawara
Tsutomu
Yui
Yurika Mori

About the author

Saori Inagaki

Founder of *iki na Joshi-Do*.
President, Thanks labo Inc.

Saori lives and works in Kamakura City, Kanagawa Prefecture, Japan.
She has been offering courses on iki na Joshi-Do since 2011. This course is designed to help people improve their happiness in a short period of time by creating a iki lifestyle. She is also active in corporate training, producing products, she is a radio personality, and lectures at elementary schools with the mission of "creating the wonderful adults that children aspire to be".

She started overseas expansion with the theme iki to the world in 2022.

iki

粋